DATE

TIME

CHARACTER

SERIES

CW00525303

☆☆☆☆

☆☆☆☆☆

COSTUME

SKETCH	ITEM	PRICE
	○	
	○	
	○	
	○	
	○	
	○	
	○	
	○	
	○	
	○	
	○	
	○	
	○	
	○	
	○	

ADDITIONAL NOTES

DATE		PROJECT RATING	

📅 DATE		PROJECT RATING	
🕐 TIME		🧵 EXPENDITURE	☆☆☆☆☆
🧸 CHARACTER		✨ DIFFICULITY	☆☆☆☆☆
🎬 SERIES		🎖 COSTS	☆☆☆☆☆

COSTUME

SKETCH	ITEM	PRICE
	○	
	○	
	○	
	○	
	○	
	○	
	○	
	○	
	○	
	○	
	○	
	○	
	○	
	○	
	○	

ADDITIONAL NOTES

DATE

TIME

CHARACTER

SERIES

PROJECT RATING

EXPENDITURE	☆☆☆☆☆
DIFFICULITY	☆☆☆☆☆
COSTS	☆☆☆☆☆

COSTUME

SKETCH	ITEM	PRICE
	○	
	○	
	○	
	○	
	○	
	○	
	○	
	○	
	○	
	○	
	○	
	○	
	○	
	○	
	○	

ADDITIONAL NOTES

DATE		PROJECT RATING	
TIME		EXPENDITURE	☆☆☆☆☆
CHARACTER		DIFFICULTY	☆☆☆☆☆
SERIES		COSTS	☆☆☆☆☆

COSTUME

SKETCH	ITEM	PRICE
	○	
	○	
	○	
	○	
	○	
	○	
	○	
	○	
	○	
	○	
	○	
	○	
	○	
	○	
	○	

ADDITIONAL NOTES

DATE		PROJECT RATING	
🕐 TIME		EXPENDITURE	☆☆☆☆☆
CHARACTER		DIFFICULITY	☆☆☆☆☆
SERIES		COSTS	☆☆☆☆☆

COSTUME

SKETCH	ITEM	PRICE
	○	
	○	
	○	
	○	
	○	
	○	
	○	
	○	
	○	
	○	
	○	
	○	
	○	
	○	
	○	

ADDITIONAL NOTES

DATE		PROJECT RATING	
TIME		EXPENDITURE	☆☆☆☆☆
CHARACTER		DIFFICULITY	☆☆☆☆☆
SERIES		COSTS	☆☆☆☆☆

COSTUME

SKETCH	ITEM	PRICE
	○	
	○	
	○	
	○	
	○	
	○	
	○	
	○	
	○	
	○	
	○	
	○	
	○	
	○	
	○	

ADDITIONAL NOTES

DATE		PROJECT RATING	
TIME		EXPENDITURE	☆☆☆☆☆
CHARACTER		DIFFICULITY	☆☆☆☆☆
SERIES		COSTS	☆☆☆☆☆

COSTUME

SKETCH	ITEM	PRICE
	○	
	○	
	○	
	○	
	○	
	○	
	○	
	○	
	○	
	○	
	○	
	○	
	○	
	○	
	○	

ADDITIONAL NOTES

DATE		PROJECT RATING	
TIME		EXPENDITURE	☆☆☆☆☆
CHARACTER		DIFFICULITY	☆☆☆☆☆
SERIES		COSTS	☆☆☆☆☆

COSTUME

SKETCH	ITEM	PRICE
	○	
	○	
	○	
	○	
	○	
	○	
	○	
	○	
	○	
	○	
	○	
	○	
	○	
	○	
	○	

ADDITIONAL NOTES

DATE		PROJECT RATING	
TIME		EXPENDITURE	☆☆☆☆☆
CHARACTER		DIFFICULITY	☆☆☆☆☆
SERIES		COSTS	☆☆☆☆☆

COSTUME

SKETCH	ITEM	PRICE
	○	
	○	
	○	
	○	
	○	
	○	
	○	
	○	
	○	
	○	
	○	
	○	
	○	
	○	
	○	

ADDITIONAL NOTES

DATE		PROJECT RATING	

DATE
TIME
CHARACTER
SERIES

PROJECT RATING

EXPENDITURE	☆☆☆☆☆
DIFFICULTY	☆☆☆☆☆
COSTS	☆☆☆☆☆

COSTUME

SKETCH	ITEM	PRICE
	○	
	○	
	○	
	○	
	○	
	○	
	○	
	○	
	○	
	○	
	○	
	○	
	○	
	○	
	○	

ADDITIONAL NOTES

▦ DATE	
🕐 TIME	
🧸 CHARACTER	
🎞 SERIES	

PROJECT RATING

🧵 EXPENDITURE	☆☆☆☆☆
👗 DIFFICULITY	☆☆☆☆☆
🏅 COSTS	☆☆☆☆☆

COSTUME

SKETCH	ITEM	PRICE
	○	
	○	
	○	
	○	
	○	
	○	
	○	
	○	
	○	
	○	
	○	
	○	
	○	
	○	
	○	

ADDITIONAL NOTES

DATE	PROJECT RATING	
TIME	EXPENDITURE	☆☆☆☆☆
CHARACTER	DIFFICULITY	☆☆☆☆☆
SERIES	COSTS	☆☆☆☆☆

COSTUME

SKETCH	ITEM	PRICE
	○	
	○	
	○	
	○	
	○	
	○	
	○	
	○	
	○	
	○	
	○	
	○	
	○	
	○	
	○	

ADDITIONAL NOTES

DATE		PROJECT RATING	

DATE

TIME

CHARACTER

SERIES

PROJECT RATING

EXPENDITURE	☆☆☆☆☆
DIFFICULITY	☆☆☆☆☆
COSTS	☆☆☆☆☆

COSTUME

SKETCH	ITEM	PRICE
	○	
	○	
	○	
	○	
	○	
	○	
	○	
	○	
	○	
	○	
	○	
	○	
	○	
	○	
	○	

ADDITIONAL NOTES

DATE		PROJECT RATING		
TIME		EXPENDITURE	☆☆☆☆☆	
CHARACTER		DIFFICULTY	☆☆☆☆☆	
SERIES		COSTS	☆☆☆☆☆	

COSTUME

SKETCH	ITEM	PRICE
	○	
	○	
	○	
	○	
	○	
	○	
	○	
	○	
	○	
	○	
	○	
	○	
	○	
	○	
	○	

ADDITIONAL NOTES

DATE		PROJECT RATING	
TIME		EXPENDITURE	☆☆☆☆☆
CHARACTER		DIFFICULITY	☆☆☆☆☆
SERIES		COSTS	☆☆☆☆☆

COSTUME

SKETCH	ITEM	PRICE
	○	
	○	
	○	
	○	
	○	
	○	
	○	
	○	
	○	
	○	
	○	
	○	
	○	
	○	
	○	

ADDITIONAL NOTES

DATE		PROJECT RATING	
TIME		EXPENDITURE	☆☆☆☆☆
CHARACTER		DIFFICULTY	☆☆☆☆☆
SERIES		COSTS	☆☆☆☆☆

COSTUME

SKETCH	ITEM	PRICE
	○	
	○	
	○	
	○	
	○	
	○	
	○	
	○	
	○	
	○	
	○	
	○	
	○	
	○	
	○	

ADDITIONAL NOTES

DATE	
TIME	
CHARACTER	
SERIES	

PROJECT RATING

EXPENDITURE	☆☆☆☆☆
DIFFICULITY	☆☆☆☆☆
COSTS	☆☆☆☆☆

COSTUME

SKETCH	ITEM	PRICE
	○	
	○	
	○	
	○	
	○	
	○	
	○	
	○	
	○	
	○	
	○	
	○	
	○	
	○	
	○	

ADDITIONAL NOTES

DATE		PROJECT RATING	

DATE

TIME

CHARACTER

SERIES

PROJECT RATING

EXPENDITURE ☆☆☆☆☆

DIFFICULITY ☆☆☆☆☆

COSTS ☆☆☆☆☆

COSTUME

SKETCH	ITEM	PRICE
	○	
	○	
	○	
	○	
	○	
	○	
	○	
	○	
	○	
	○	
	○	
	○	
	○	
	○	
	○	

ADDITIONAL NOTES

DATE	PROJECT RATING	
TIME	EXPENDITURE	☆☆☆☆☆
CHARACTER	DIFFICULITY	☆☆☆☆☆
SERIES	COSTS	☆☆☆☆☆

COSTUME

SKETCH	ITEM	PRICE
	○	
	○	
	○	
	○	
	○	
	○	
	○	
	○	
	○	
	○	
	○	
	○	
	○	
	○	
	○	

ADDITIONAL NOTES

📅 DATE		**PROJECT RATING**	
🕐 TIME		🧵 EXPENDITURE	☆☆☆☆☆
🐻 CHARACTER		🎎 DIFFICULTY	☆☆☆☆☆
🎬 SERIES		🏅 COSTS	☆☆☆☆☆

COSTUME

SKETCH	ITEM	PRICE
	◯	
	◯	
	◯	
	◯	
	◯	
	◯	
	◯	
	◯	
	◯	
	◯	
	◯	
	◯	
	◯	
	◯	
	◯	

ADDITIONAL NOTES

DATE		PROJECT RATING		
TIME		EXPENDITURE	☆☆☆☆☆	
CHARACTER		DIFFICULITY	☆☆☆☆☆	
SERIES		COSTS	☆☆☆☆☆	

COSTUME

SKETCH	ITEM	PRICE
	○	
	○	
	○	
	○	
	○	
	○	
	○	
	○	
	○	
	○	
	○	
	○	
	○	
	○	
	○	

ADDITIONAL NOTES

DATE		PROJECT RATING	
TIME		EXPENDITURE	☆☆☆☆☆
CHARACTER		DIFFICULITY	☆☆☆☆☆
SERIES		COSTS	☆☆☆☆☆

COSTUME

SKETCH	ITEM	PRICE
	○	
	○	
	○	
	○	
	○	
	○	
	○	
	○	
	○	
	○	
	○	
	○	
	○	
	○	
	○	

ADDITIONAL NOTES

DATE		PROJECT RATING	
TIME		EXPENDITURE	☆☆☆☆☆
CHARACTER		DIFFICULITY	☆☆☆☆☆
SERIES		COSTS	☆☆☆☆☆

COSTUME

SKETCH	ITEM	PRICE
	○	
	○	
	○	
	○	
	○	
	○	
	○	
	○	
	○	
	○	
	○	
	○	
	○	
	○	
	○	

ADDITIONAL NOTES

DATE	PROJECT RATING	
TIME	EXPENDITURE	☆☆☆☆☆
CHARACTER	DIFFICULITY	☆☆☆☆☆
SERIES	COSTS	☆☆☆☆☆

COSTUME

SKETCH	ITEM	PRICE
	○	
	○	
	○	
	○	
	○	
	○	
	○	
	○	
	○	
	○	
	○	
	○	
	○	
	○	
	○	

ADDITIONAL NOTES

DATE

TIME

CHARACTER

SERIES

PROJECT RATING

EXPENDITURE	☆☆☆☆☆
DIFFICULTY	☆☆☆☆☆
COSTS	☆☆☆☆☆

COSTUME

SKETCH	ITEM	PRICE
	○	
	○	
	○	
	○	
	○	
	○	
	○	
	○	
	○	
	○	
	○	
	○	
	○	
	○	
	○	

ADDITIONAL NOTES

DATE		PROJECT RATING	
🗓 DATE		✂ EXPENDITURE	☆☆☆☆☆
🕐 TIME		👗 DIFFICULITY	☆☆☆☆☆
🐻 CHARACTER		🏅 COSTS	☆☆☆☆☆
🎬 SERIES			

COSTUME

SKETCH	ITEM	PRICE
	○	
	○	
	○	
	○	
	○	
	○	
	○	
	○	
	○	
	○	
	○	
	○	
	○	
	○	
	○	

ADDITIONAL NOTES

	DATE
	TIME
	CHARACTER
	SERIES

PROJECT RATING

	EXPENDITURE	☆☆☆☆☆
	DIFFICULITY	☆☆☆☆☆
	COSTS	☆☆☆☆☆

COSTUME

SKETCH	ITEM	PRICE
	○	
	○	
	○	
	○	
	○	
	○	
	○	
	○	
	○	
	○	
	○	
	○	
	○	
	○	
	○	

ADDITIONAL NOTES

DATE		PROJECT RATING	

DATE

TIME

CHARACTER

SERIES

PROJECT RATING

EXPENDITURE ☆☆☆☆☆

DIFFICULITY ☆☆☆☆☆

COSTS ☆☆☆☆☆

COSTUME

SKETCH	ITEM	PRICE
	○	
	○	
	○	
	○	
	○	
	○	
	○	
	○	
	○	
	○	
	○	
	○	
	○	
	○	
	○	

ADDITIONAL NOTES

DATE		PROJECT RATING	

📅 DATE
🕐 TIME
🧸 CHARACTER
🎬 SERIES

PROJECT RATING	
🧵 EXPENDITURE	☆☆☆☆☆
👗 DIFFICULITY	☆☆☆☆☆
🎖 COSTS	☆☆☆☆☆

COSTUME

SKETCH	ITEM	PRICE
	○	
	○	
	○	
	○	
	○	
	○	
	○	
	○	
	○	
	○	
	○	
	○	
	○	
	○	
	○	

ADDITIONAL NOTES

	DATE
	TIME
	CHARACTER
	SERIES

PROJECT RATING

	EXPENDITURE	☆☆☆☆☆
	DIFFICULITY	☆☆☆☆☆
	COSTS	☆☆☆☆☆

COSTUME

SKETCH	ITEM	PRICE
	○	
	○	
	○	
	○	
	○	
	○	
	○	
	○	
	○	
	○	
	○	
	○	
	○	
	○	
	○	

ADDITIONAL NOTES

DATE

TIME

CHARACTER

SERIES

PROJECT RATING

EXPENDITURE	☆☆☆☆☆
DIFFICULITY	☆☆☆☆☆
COSTS	☆☆☆☆☆

COSTUME

SKETCH	ITEM	PRICE
	○	
	○	
	○	
	○	
	○	
	○	
	○	
	○	
	○	
	○	
	○	
	○	
	○	
	○	
	○	

ADDITIONAL NOTES

DATE	PROJECT RATING		
TIME	EXPENDITURE	☆☆☆☆☆	
CHARACTER	DIFFICULITY	☆☆☆☆☆	
SERIES	COSTS	☆☆☆☆☆	

COSTUME

SKETCH	ITEM	PRICE
	○	
	○	
	○	
	○	
	○	
	○	
	○	
	○	
	○	
	○	
	○	
	○	
	○	
	○	
	○	

ADDITIONAL NOTES

DATE		PROJECT RATING	
TIME		EXPENDITURE	☆☆☆☆☆
CHARACTER		DIFFICULITY	☆☆☆☆☆
SERIES		COSTS	☆☆☆☆☆

COSTUME

SKETCH	ITEM	PRICE
	○	
	○	
	○	
	○	
	○	
	○	
	○	
	○	
	○	
	○	
	○	
	○	
	○	
	○	
	○	

ADDITIONAL NOTES

📅 DATE		PROJECT RATING	
🕐 TIME		🧵 EXPENDITURE	☆☆☆☆☆
🧸 CHARACTER		💃 DIFFICULTY	☆☆☆☆☆
🎬 SERIES		🏅 COSTS	☆☆☆☆☆

COSTUME

SKETCH	ITEM	PRICE
	○	
	○	
	○	
	○	
	○	
	○	
	○	
	○	
	○	
	○	
	○	
	○	
	○	
	○	
	○	

ADDITIONAL NOTES

DATE		PROJECT RATING	
TIME		EXPENDITURE	☆☆☆☆☆
CHARACTER		DIFFICULITY	☆☆☆☆☆
SERIES		COSTS	☆☆☆☆☆

COSTUME

SKETCH	ITEM	PRICE
	○	
	○	
	○	
	○	
	○	
	○	
	○	
	○	
	○	
	○	
	○	
	○	
	○	
	○	
	○	

ADDITIONAL NOTES

DATE		PROJECT RATING	

📅 **DATE**
🕐 **TIME**
🐾 **CHARACTER**
🎬 **SERIES**

PROJECT RATING

🧵 EXPENDITURE	☆☆☆☆☆
👗 DIFFICULITY	☆☆☆☆☆
🏅 COSTS	☆☆☆☆☆

COSTUME

SKETCH	ITEM	PRICE
	○	
	○	
	○	
	○	
	○	
	○	
	○	
	○	
	○	
	○	
	○	
	○	
	○	
	○	
	○	

ADDITIONAL NOTES

DATE	PROJECT RATING	
TIME	EXPENDITURE	☆☆☆☆☆
CHARACTER	DIFFICULITY	☆☆☆☆☆
SERIES	COSTS	☆☆☆☆☆

COSTUME

SKETCH	ITEM	PRICE
	○	
	○	
	○	
	○	
	○	
	○	
	○	
	○	
	○	
	○	
	○	
	○	
	○	
	○	
	○	

ADDITIONAL NOTES

DATE
TIME
CHARACTER
SERIES

PROJECT RATING

EXPENDITURE	☆☆☆☆☆
DIFFICULTY	☆☆☆☆☆
COSTS	☆☆☆☆☆

COSTUME

SKETCH	ITEM	PRICE
	○	
	○	
	○	
	○	
	○	
	○	
	○	
	○	
	○	
	○	
	○	
	○	
	○	
	○	
	○	

ADDITIONAL NOTES

DATE	PROJECT RATING		

DATE		PROJECT RATING	
TIME		EXPENDITURE	☆☆☆☆☆
CHARACTER		DIFFICULITY	☆☆☆☆☆
SERIES		COSTS	☆☆☆☆☆

COSTUME

SKETCH	ITEM	PRICE
	○	
	○	
	○	
	○	
	○	
	○	
	○	
	○	
	○	
	○	
	○	
	○	
	○	
	○	
	○	

ADDITIONAL NOTES

DATE		PROJECT RATING	
TIME		EXPENDITURE	☆☆☆☆☆
CHARACTER		DIFFICULTY	☆☆☆☆☆
SERIES		COSTS	☆☆☆☆☆

COSTUME

SKETCH	ITEM	PRICE
	○	
	○	
	○	
	○	
	○	
	○	
	○	
	○	
	○	
	○	
	○	
	○	
	○	
	○	
	○	

ADDITIONAL NOTES

| DATE |
| TIME |
| CHARACTER |
| SERIES |

PROJECT RATING

EXPENDITURE	☆☆☆☆☆
DIFFICULITY	☆☆☆☆☆
COSTS	☆☆☆☆☆

COSTUME

SKETCH	ITEM	PRICE
	○	
	○	
	○	
	○	
	○	
	○	
	○	
	○	
	○	
	○	
	○	
	○	
	○	
	○	
	○	

ADDITIONAL NOTES

DATE		PROJECT RATING	

DATE

TIME

CHARACTER

SERIES

PROJECT RATING

EXPENDITURE ☆☆☆☆☆

DIFFICULITY ☆☆☆☆☆

COSTS ☆☆☆☆☆

COSTUME

SKETCH	ITEM	PRICE
	○	
	○	
	○	
	○	
	○	
	○	
	○	
	○	
	○	
	○	
	○	
	○	
	○	
	○	
	○	

ADDITIONAL NOTES

DATE		PROJECT RATING	
TIME		EXPENDITURE	☆☆☆☆☆
CHARACTER		DIFFICULITY	☆☆☆☆☆
SERIES		COSTS	☆☆☆☆☆

COSTUME

SKETCH	ITEM	PRICE
	○	
	○	
	○	
	○	
	○	
	○	
	○	
	○	
	○	
	○	
	○	
	○	
	○	
	○	
	○	

ADDITIONAL NOTES

DATE		PROJECT RATING	
TIME		EXPENDITURE	☆☆☆☆☆
CHARACTER		DIFFICULTY	☆☆☆☆☆
SERIES		COSTS	☆☆☆☆☆

COSTUME

SKETCH	ITEM	PRICE
	○	
	○	
	○	
	○	
	○	
	○	
	○	
	○	
	○	
	○	
	○	
	○	
	○	
	○	
	○	

ADDITIONAL NOTES

DATE		PROJECT RATING	
TIME		EXPENDITURE	☆☆☆☆☆
CHARACTER		DIFFICULITY	☆☆☆☆☆
SERIES		COSTS	☆☆☆☆☆

COSTUME

SKETCH	ITEM	PRICE
	○	
	○	
	○	
	○	
	○	
	○	
	○	
	○	
	○	
	○	
	○	
	○	
	○	
	○	
	○	

ADDITIONAL NOTES

DATE		PROJECT RATING		
TIME		EXPENDITURE	☆☆☆☆☆	
CHARACTER		DIFFICULITY	☆☆☆☆☆	
SERIES		COSTS	☆☆☆☆☆	

COSTUME

SKETCH	ITEM	PRICE
	○	
	○	
	○	
	○	
	○	
	○	
	○	
	○	
	○	
	○	
	○	
	○	
	○	
	○	
	○	

ADDITIONAL NOTES

DATE	PROJECT RATING		
TIME	EXPENDITURE	☆☆☆☆☆	
CHARACTER	DIFFICULITY	☆☆☆☆☆	
SERIES	COSTS	☆☆☆☆☆	

COSTUME

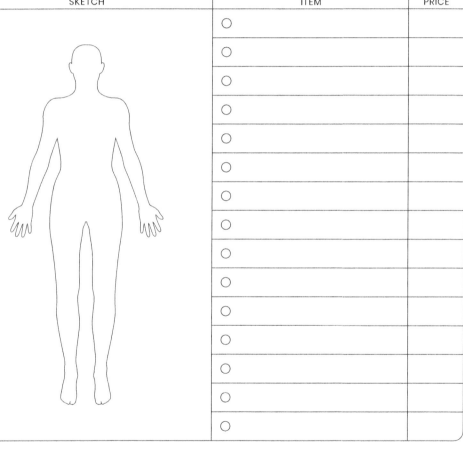

SKETCH	ITEM	PRICE
	○	
	○	
	○	
	○	
	○	
	○	
	○	
	○	
	○	
	○	
	○	
	○	
	○	
	○	
	○	

ADDITIONAL NOTES

DATE		PROJECT RATING		
TIME		EXPENDITURE	☆☆☆☆☆	
CHARACTER		DIFFICULITY	☆☆☆☆☆	
SERIES		COSTS	☆☆☆☆☆	

COSTUME

SKETCH	ITEM	PRICE
	○	
	○	
	○	
	○	
	○	
	○	
	○	
	○	
	○	
	○	
	○	
	○	
	○	
	○	
	○	

ADDITIONAL NOTES

DATE		PROJECT RATING		
TIME		EXPENDITURE	☆☆☆☆☆	
CHARACTER		DIFFICULITY	☆☆☆☆☆	
SERIES		COSTS	☆☆☆☆☆	

COSTUME

SKETCH	ITEM	PRICE
	○	
	○	
	○	
	○	
	○	
	○	
	○	
	○	
	○	
	○	
	○	
	○	
	○	
	○	
	○	

ADDITIONAL NOTES

DATE		PROJECT RATING		
TIME		EXPENDITURE		☆☆☆☆☆
CHARACTER		DIFFICULITY		☆☆☆☆☆
SERIES		COSTS		☆☆☆☆☆

COSTUME

SKETCH	ITEM	PRICE
	○	
	○	
	○	
	○	
	○	
	○	
	○	
	○	
	○	
	○	
	○	
	○	
	○	
	○	
	○	

ADDITIONAL NOTES

DATE		PROJECT RATING	
TIME		EXPENDITURE	☆☆☆☆☆
CHARACTER		DIFFICULITY	☆☆☆☆☆
SERIES		COSTS	☆☆☆☆☆

COSTUME

SKETCH	ITEM	PRICE
	○	
	○	
	○	
	○	
	○	
	○	
	○	
	○	
	○	
	○	
	○	
	○	
	○	
	○	
	○	

ADDITIONAL NOTES

DATE		PROJECT RATING	
TIME		EXPENDITURE	☆☆☆☆☆
CHARACTER		DIFFICULTY	☆☆☆☆☆
SERIES		COSTS	☆☆☆☆☆

COSTUME

SKETCH	ITEM	PRICE
	○	
	○	
	○	
	○	
	○	
	○	
	○	
	○	
	○	
	○	
	○	
	○	
	○	
	○	
	○	

ADDITIONAL NOTES

DATE		PROJECT RATING	
TIME		EXPENDITURE	☆☆☆☆☆
CHARACTER		DIFFICULTY	☆☆☆☆☆
SERIES		COSTS	☆☆☆☆☆

COSTUME

SKETCH	ITEM	PRICE
	○	
	○	
	○	
	○	
	○	
	○	
	○	
	○	
	○	
	○	
	○	
	○	
	○	
	○	
	○	

ADDITIONAL NOTES

DATE		PROJECT RATING	
TIME		EXPENDITURE	☆☆☆☆☆
CHARACTER		DIFFICULITY	☆☆☆☆☆
SERIES		COSTS	☆☆☆☆☆

COSTUME

SKETCH	ITEM	PRICE
	○	
	○	
	○	
	○	
	○	
	○	
	○	
	○	
	○	
	○	
	○	
	○	
	○	
	○	
	○	

ADDITIONAL NOTES

DATE		PROJECT RATING	
TIME		EXPENDITURE	☆☆☆☆☆
CHARACTER		DIFFICULITY	☆☆☆☆☆
SERIES		COSTS	☆☆☆☆☆

COSTUME

SKETCH	ITEM	PRICE
	○	
	○	
	○	
	○	
	○	
	○	
	○	
	○	
	○	
	○	
	○	
	○	
	○	
	○	
	○	

ADDITIONAL NOTES

DATE		PROJECT RATING	

📅 **DATE**

🕐 **TIME**

🐻 **CHARACTER**

🎬 **SERIES**

PROJECT RATING

🧵 EXPENDITURE ☆☆☆☆☆

👗 DIFFICULITY ☆☆☆☆☆

🎖️ COSTS ☆☆☆☆☆

COSTUME

SKETCH	ITEM	PRICE
	◯	
	◯	
	◯	
	◯	
	◯	
	◯	
	◯	
	◯	
	◯	
	◯	
	◯	
	◯	
	◯	
	◯	
	◯	

ADDITIONAL NOTES

DATE		PROJECT RATING	

DATE	
TIME	
CHARACTER	
SERIES	

PROJECT RATING	
EXPENDITURE	☆☆☆☆☆
DIFFICULITY	☆☆☆☆☆
COSTS	☆☆☆☆☆

COSTUME

SKETCH		ITEM	PRICE
	○		
	○		
	○		
	○		
	○		
	○		
	○		
	○		
	○		
	○		
	○		
	○		
	○		
	○		
	○		

ADDITIONAL NOTES

DATE		PROJECT RATING		
TIME		EXPENDITURE		☆☆☆☆☆
CHARACTER		DIFFICULTY		☆☆☆☆☆
SERIES		COSTS		☆☆☆☆☆

COSTUME

SKETCH	ITEM	PRICE
	○	
	○	
	○	
	○	
	○	
	○	
	○	
	○	
	○	
	○	
	○	
	○	
	○	
	○	
	○	

ADDITIONAL NOTES

DATE
TIME
CHARACTER
SERIES

PROJECT RATING

EXPENDITURE	☆☆☆☆☆
DIFFICULITY	☆☆☆☆☆
COSTS	☆☆☆☆☆

COSTUME

SKETCH	ITEM	PRICE
	○	
	○	
	○	
	○	
	○	
	○	
	○	
	○	
	○	
	○	
	○	
	○	
	○	
	○	
	○	

ADDITIONAL NOTES

DATE		PROJECT RATING	

DATE

TIME

CHARACTER

SERIES

PROJECT RATING

EXPENDITURE ☆☆☆☆☆

DIFFICULITY ☆☆☆☆☆

COSTS ☆☆☆☆☆

COSTUME

SKETCH	ITEM	PRICE
	○	
	○	
	○	
	○	
	○	
	○	
	○	
	○	
	○	
	○	
	○	
	○	
	○	
	○	
	○	

ADDITIONAL NOTES

DATE		PROJECT RATING	

DATE

TIME

CHARACTER

SERIES

PROJECT RATING

EXPENDITURE ☆☆☆☆☆

DIFFICULITY ☆☆☆☆☆

COSTS ☆☆☆☆☆

COSTUME

SKETCH	ITEM	PRICE
	○	
	○	
	○	
	○	
	○	
	○	
	○	
	○	
	○	
	○	
	○	
	○	
	○	
	○	
	○	

ADDITIONAL NOTES

	DATE
	TIME
	CHARACTER
	SERIES

PROJECT RATING

	EXPENDITURE	☆☆☆☆☆
	DIFFICULITY	☆☆☆☆☆
	COSTS	☆☆☆☆☆

COSTUME

SKETCH	ITEM	PRICE
	○	
	○	
	○	
	○	
	○	
	○	
	○	
	○	
	○	
	○	
	○	
	○	
	○	
	○	
	○	

ADDITIONAL NOTES

DATE		PROJECT RATING	
TIME		EXPENDITURE	☆☆☆☆☆
CHARACTER		DIFFICULITY	☆☆☆☆☆
SERIES		COSTS	☆☆☆☆☆

COSTUME

SKETCH	ITEM	PRICE
	○	
	○	
	○	
	○	
	○	
	○	
	○	
	○	
	○	
	○	
	○	
	○	
	○	
	○	
	○	

ADDITIONAL NOTES

DATE		PROJECT RATING	
TIME		EXPENDITURE	☆☆☆☆☆
CHARACTER		DIFFICULTY	☆☆☆☆☆
SERIES		COSTS	☆☆☆☆☆

COSTUME

SKETCH	ITEM	PRICE
	○	
	○	
	○	
	○	
	○	
	○	
	○	
	○	
	○	
	○	
	○	
	○	
	○	
	○	
	○	

ADDITIONAL NOTES

DATE	PROJECT RATING		

DATE

TIME

CHARACTER

SERIES

PROJECT RATING

EXPENDITURE	☆☆☆☆☆
DIFFICULITY	☆☆☆☆☆
COSTS	☆☆☆☆☆

COSTUME

SKETCH	ITEM	PRICE
	○	
	○	
	○	
	○	
	○	
	○	
	○	
	○	
	○	
	○	
	○	
	○	
	○	
	○	
	○	

ADDITIONAL NOTES

DATE		PROJECT RATING	
TIME		EXPENDITURE	☆☆☆☆☆
CHARACTER		DIFFICULITY	☆☆☆☆☆
SERIES		COSTS	☆☆☆☆☆

COSTUME

SKETCH	ITEM	PRICE
	○	
	○	
	○	
	○	
	○	
	○	
	○	
	○	
	○	
	○	
	○	
	○	
	○	
	○	
	○	

ADDITIONAL NOTES

DATE		PROJECT RATING	
TIME		EXPENDITURE	☆☆☆☆☆
CHARACTER		DIFFICULITY	☆☆☆☆☆
SERIES		COSTS	☆☆☆☆☆

COSTUME

SKETCH	ITEM	PRICE
	○	
	○	
	○	
	○	
	○	
	○	
	○	
	○	
	○	
	○	
	○	
	○	
	○	
	○	
	○	

ADDITIONAL NOTES

DATE	PROJECT RATING	
TIME	EXPENDITURE	☆☆☆☆☆
CHARACTER	DIFFICULITY	☆☆☆☆☆
SERIES	COSTS	☆☆☆☆☆

COSTUME

SKETCH	ITEM	PRICE
	○	
	○	
	○	
	○	
	○	
	○	
	○	
	○	
	○	
	○	
	○	
	○	
	○	
	○	
	○	

ADDITIONAL NOTES

DATE		PROJECT RATING	
🕐 TIME		✂️ EXPENDITURE	☆☆☆☆☆
👘 CHARACTER		✨ DIFFICULITY	☆☆☆☆☆
🎬 SERIES		🏅 COSTS	☆☆☆☆☆

COSTUME

SKETCH	ITEM	PRICE
	○	
	○	
	○	
	○	
	○	
	○	
	○	
	○	
	○	
	○	
	○	
	○	
	○	
	○	
	○	

ADDITIONAL NOTES

DATE		PROJECT RATING	
TIME		EXPENDITURE	☆☆☆☆☆
CHARACTER		DIFFICULITY	☆☆☆☆☆
SERIES		COSTS	☆☆☆☆☆

COSTUME

SKETCH	ITEM	PRICE
	○	
	○	
	○	
	○	
	○	
	○	
	○	
	○	
	○	
	○	
	○	
	○	
	○	
	○	
	○	

ADDITIONAL NOTES

DATE	PROJECT RATING		

DATE		PROJECT RATING	
TIME	EXPENDITURE	☆☆☆☆☆	
CHARACTER	DIFFICULITY	☆☆☆☆☆	
SERIES	COSTS	☆☆☆☆☆	

COSTUME

SKETCH	ITEM	PRICE
	○	
	○	
	○	
	○	
	○	
	○	
	○	
	○	
	○	
	○	
	○	
	○	
	○	
	○	
	○	

ADDITIONAL NOTES

DATE	PROJECT RATING		

📅 DATE	
🕐 TIME	
🎎 CHARACTER	
🎬 SERIES	

PROJECT RATING

🧵 EXPENDITURE	☆☆☆☆☆
🎀 DIFFICULITY	☆☆☆☆☆
🎖️ COSTS	☆☆☆☆☆

COSTUME

SKETCH	ITEM	PRICE
	○	
	○	
	○	
	○	
	○	
	○	
	○	
	○	
	○	
	○	
	○	
	○	
	○	
	○	
	○	

ADDITIONAL NOTES

DATE	PROJECT RATING		
TIME	EXPENDITURE	☆☆☆☆☆	
CHARACTER	DIFFICULITY	☆☆☆☆☆	
SERIES	COSTS	☆☆☆☆☆	

COSTUME

SKETCH	ITEM	PRICE
	○	
	○	
	○	
	○	
	○	
	○	
	○	
	○	
	○	
	○	
	○	
	○	
	○	
	○	
	○	

ADDITIONAL NOTES

DATE		PROJECT RATING		
TIME		EXPENDITURE		☆☆☆☆☆
CHARACTER		DIFFICULITY		☆☆☆☆☆
SERIES		COSTS		☆☆☆☆☆

COSTUME

SKETCH	ITEM	PRICE
	○	
	○	
	○	
	○	
	○	
	○	
	○	
	○	
	○	
	○	
	○	
	○	
	○	
	○	
	○	

ADDITIONAL NOTES

DATE		PROJECT RATING	

DATE

TIME

CHARACTER

SERIES

PROJECT RATING

EXPENDITURE ☆☆☆☆☆

DIFFICULITY ☆☆☆☆☆

COSTS ☆☆☆☆☆

COSTUME

SKETCH	ITEM	PRICE
	○	
	○	
	○	
	○	
	○	
	○	
	○	
	○	
	○	
	○	
	○	
	○	
	○	
	○	
	○	

ADDITIONAL NOTES

DATE		PROJECT RATING		
TIME		EXPENDITURE	☆☆☆☆☆	
CHARACTER		DIFFICULITY	☆☆☆☆☆	
SERIES		COSTS	☆☆☆☆☆	

COSTUME

SKETCH	ITEM	PRICE
	○	
	○	
	○	
	○	
	○	
	○	
	○	
	○	
	○	
	○	
	○	
	○	
	○	
	○	
	○	

ADDITIONAL NOTES

DATE		PROJECT RATING	
TIME		EXPENDITURE	☆☆☆☆☆
CHARACTER		DIFFICULITY	☆☆☆☆☆
SERIES		COSTS	☆☆☆☆☆

COSTUME

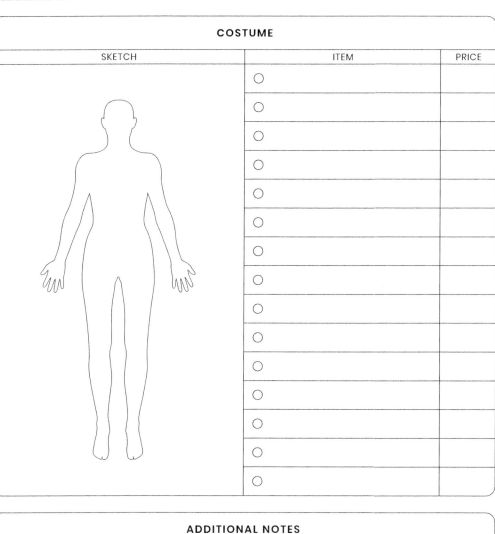

SKETCH	ITEM	PRICE
	○	
	○	
	○	
	○	
	○	
	○	
	○	
	○	
	○	
	○	
	○	
	○	
	○	
	○	
	○	

ADDITIONAL NOTES

DATE	PROJECT RATING		
TIME	EXPENDITURE	☆☆☆☆☆	
CHARACTER	DIFFICULITY	☆☆☆☆☆	
SERIES	COSTS	☆☆☆☆☆	

COSTUME

SKETCH	ITEM	PRICE
	○	
	○	
	○	
	○	
	○	
	○	
	○	
	○	
	○	
	○	
	○	
	○	
	○	
	○	
	○	

ADDITIONAL NOTES

DATE		PROJECT RATING	
TIME		EXPENDITURE	☆☆☆☆☆
CHARACTER		DIFFICULITY	☆☆☆☆☆
SERIES		COSTS	☆☆☆☆☆

COSTUME

SKETCH	ITEM	PRICE
	○	
	○	
	○	
	○	
	○	
	○	
	○	
	○	
	○	
	○	
	○	
	○	
	○	
	○	
	○	

ADDITIONAL NOTES

DATE		PROJECT RATING	
TIME		EXPENDITURE	☆☆☆☆☆
CHARACTER		DIFFICULITY	☆☆☆☆☆
SERIES		COSTS	☆☆☆☆☆

COSTUME

SKETCH	ITEM	PRICE
	○	
	○	
	○	
	○	
	○	
	○	
	○	
	○	
	○	
	○	
	○	
	○	
	○	
	○	
	○	

ADDITIONAL NOTES

DATE		PROJECT RATING		
TIME		EXPENDITURE	☆☆☆☆☆	
CHARACTER		DIFFICULITY	☆☆☆☆☆	
SERIES		COSTS	☆☆☆☆☆	

COSTUME

SKETCH	ITEM	PRICE
	○	
	○	
	○	
	○	
	○	
	○	
	○	
	○	
	○	
	○	
	○	
	○	
	○	
	○	
	○	

ADDITIONAL NOTES

DATE		PROJECT RATING		
TIME		EXPENDITURE	☆☆☆☆☆	
CHARACTER		DIFFICULITY	☆☆☆☆☆	
SERIES		COSTS	☆☆☆☆☆	

COSTUME

SKETCH	ITEM	PRICE
	○	
	○	
	○	
	○	
	○	
	○	
	○	
	○	
	○	
	○	
	○	
	○	
	○	
	○	
	○	

ADDITIONAL NOTES

DATE		PROJECT RATING	
TIME		EXPENDITURE	☆☆☆☆☆
CHARACTER		DIFFICULITY	☆☆☆☆☆
SERIES		COSTS	☆☆☆☆☆

COSTUME

SKETCH	ITEM	PRICE
	○	
	○	
	○	
	○	
	○	
	○	
	○	
	○	
	○	
	○	
	○	
	○	
	○	
	○	
	○	

ADDITIONAL NOTES

	DATE
	TIME
	CHARACTER
	SERIES

PROJECT RATING

EXPENDITURE	☆☆☆☆☆
DIFFICULTY	☆☆☆☆☆
COSTS	☆☆☆☆☆

COSTUME

SKETCH	ITEM	PRICE
	○	
	○	
	○	
	○	
	○	
	○	
	○	
	○	
	○	
	○	
	○	
	○	
	○	
	○	
	○	

ADDITIONAL NOTES

DATE		PROJECT RATING	
TIME		EXPENDITURE	☆☆☆☆☆
CHARACTER		DIFFICULITY	☆☆☆☆☆
SERIES		COSTS	☆☆☆☆☆

COSTUME

SKETCH	ITEM	PRICE
	○	
	○	
	○	
	○	
	○	
	○	
	○	
	○	
	○	
	○	
	○	
	○	
	○	
	○	
	○	

ADDITIONAL NOTES

DATE	PROJECT RATING	
TIME	EXPENDITURE	☆☆☆☆☆
CHARACTER	DIFFICULTY	☆☆☆☆☆
SERIES	COSTS	☆☆☆☆☆

COSTUME

SKETCH	ITEM	PRICE
	○	
	○	
	○	
	○	
	○	
	○	
	○	
	○	
	○	
	○	
	○	
	○	
	○	
	○	
	○	

ADDITIONAL NOTES

DATE		PROJECT RATING		
TIME		EXPENDITURE	☆☆☆☆☆	
CHARACTER		DIFFICULITY	☆☆☆☆☆	
SERIES		COSTS	☆☆☆☆☆	

COSTUME

SKETCH	ITEM	PRICE
	○	
	○	
	○	
	○	
	○	
	○	
	○	
	○	
	○	
	○	
	○	
	○	
	○	
	○	
	○	

ADDITIONAL NOTES

DATE		PROJECT RATING	
TIME		EXPENDITURE	☆☆☆☆☆
CHARACTER		DIFFICULTY	☆☆☆☆☆
SERIES		COSTS	☆☆☆☆☆

COSTUME

SKETCH	ITEM	PRICE
	○	
	○	
	○	
	○	
	○	
	○	
	○	
	○	
	○	
	○	
	○	
	○	
	○	
	○	
	○	

ADDITIONAL NOTES

DATE	PROJECT RATING		
TIME	EXPENDITURE	☆☆☆☆☆	
CHARACTER	DIFFICULITY	☆☆☆☆☆	
SERIES	COSTS	☆☆☆☆☆	

COSTUME

SKETCH	ITEM	PRICE
	○	
	○	
	○	
	○	
	○	
	○	
	○	
	○	
	○	
	○	
	○	
	○	
	○	
	○	
	○	

ADDITIONAL NOTES

DATE		PROJECT RATING		

📅 DATE
🕐 TIME
👹 CHARACTER
🎬 SERIES

PROJECT RATING

🧵 EXPENDITURE	☆☆☆☆☆
👗 DIFFICULTY	☆☆☆☆☆
🏅 COSTS	☆☆☆☆☆

COSTUME

SKETCH	ITEM	PRICE
	○	
	○	
	○	
	○	
	○	
	○	
	○	
	○	
	○	
	○	
	○	
	○	
	○	
	○	
	○	

ADDITIONAL NOTES

DATE		PROJECT RATING	
TIME		EXPENDITURE	☆☆☆☆☆
CHARACTER		DIFFICULITY	☆☆☆☆☆
SERIES		COSTS	☆☆☆☆☆

COSTUME

SKETCH	ITEM	PRICE
	○	
	○	
	○	
	○	
	○	
	○	
	○	
	○	
	○	
	○	
	○	
	○	
	○	
	○	
	○	

ADDITIONAL NOTES

DATE	PROJECT RATING		

DATE			PROJECT RATING	
TIME		EXPENDITURE	☆☆☆☆☆	
CHARACTER		DIFFICULTY	☆☆☆☆☆	
SERIES		COSTS	☆☆☆☆☆	

COSTUME

SKETCH	ITEM	PRICE
	○	
	○	
	○	
	○	
	○	
	○	
	○	
	○	
	○	
	○	
	○	
	○	
	○	
	○	
	○	

ADDITIONAL NOTES

DATE		PROJECT RATING	
TIME		EXPENDITURE	☆☆☆☆☆
CHARACTER		DIFFICULITY	☆☆☆☆☆
SERIES		COSTS	☆☆☆☆☆

COSTUME

SKETCH	ITEM	PRICE
	○	
	○	
	○	
	○	
	○	
	○	
	○	
	○	
	○	
	○	
	○	
	○	
	○	
	○	
	○	

ADDITIONAL NOTES

DATE		PROJECT RATING	

DATE

TIME

CHARACTER

SERIES

PROJECT RATING

EXPENDITURE	☆☆☆☆☆
DIFFICULTY	☆☆☆☆☆
COSTS	☆☆☆☆☆

COSTUME

SKETCH	ITEM	PRICE
	○	
	○	
	○	
	○	
	○	
	○	
	○	
	○	
	○	
	○	
	○	
	○	
	○	
	○	
	○	

ADDITIONAL NOTES

DATE		PROJECT RATING	
TIME		EXPENDITURE	☆☆☆☆☆
CHARACTER		DIFFICULITY	☆☆☆☆☆
SERIES		COSTS	☆☆☆☆☆

COSTUME

SKETCH	ITEM	PRICE
	○	
	○	
	○	
	○	
	○	
	○	
	○	
	○	
	○	
	○	
	○	
	○	
	○	
	○	
	○	

ADDITIONAL NOTES

DATE	PROJECT RATING	
TIME	EXPENDITURE	☆☆☆☆☆
CHARACTER	DIFFICULITY	☆☆☆☆☆
SERIES	COSTS	☆☆☆☆☆

COSTUME

SKETCH	ITEM	PRICE
	○	
	○	
	○	
	○	
	○	
	○	
	○	
	○	
	○	
	○	
	○	
	○	
	○	
	○	
	○	

ADDITIONAL NOTES

DATE		PROJECT RATING	
TIME		EXPENDITURE	☆☆☆☆☆
CHARACTER		DIFFICULITY	☆☆☆☆☆
SERIES		COSTS	☆☆☆☆☆

COSTUME

SKETCH	ITEM	PRICE
	○	
	○	
	○	
	○	
	○	
	○	
	○	
	○	
	○	
	○	
	○	
	○	
	○	
	○	
	○	

ADDITIONAL NOTES

DATE	PROJECT RATING		
TIME	EXPENDITURE	☆☆☆☆☆	
CHARACTER	DIFFICULTY	☆☆☆☆☆	
SERIES	COSTS	☆☆☆☆☆	

COSTUME

SKETCH	ITEM	PRICE
	○	
	○	
	○	
	○	
	○	
	○	
	○	
	○	
	○	
	○	
	○	
	○	
	○	
	○	
	○	

ADDITIONAL NOTES

DATE		PROJECT RATING	
TIME		EXPENDITURE	☆☆☆☆☆
CHARACTER		DIFFICULITY	☆☆☆☆☆
SERIES		COSTS	☆☆☆☆☆

COSTUME

SKETCH	ITEM	PRICE
	○	
	○	
	○	
	○	
	○	
	○	
	○	
	○	
	○	
	○	
	○	
	○	
	○	
	○	
	○	

ADDITIONAL NOTES

DATE		PROJECT RATING	
TIME		EXPENDITURE	☆☆☆☆☆
CHARACTER		DIFFICULTY	☆☆☆☆☆
SERIES		COSTS	☆☆☆☆☆

COSTUME

SKETCH	ITEM	PRICE
	○	
	○	
	○	
	○	
	○	
	○	
	○	
	○	
	○	
	○	
	○	
	○	
	○	
	○	
	○	

ADDITIONAL NOTES

DATE		PROJECT RATING	

DATE

TIME

CHARACTER

SERIES

PROJECT RATING

EXPENDITURE	☆☆☆☆☆
DIFFICULITY	☆☆☆☆☆
COSTS	☆☆☆☆☆

COSTUME

SKETCH	ITEM	PRICE
	○	
	○	
	○	
	○	
	○	
	○	
	○	
	○	
	○	
	○	
	○	
	○	
	○	
	○	
	○	

ADDITIONAL NOTES

DATE		PROJECT RATING	
TIME		EXPENDITURE	☆☆☆☆☆
CHARACTER		DIFFICULITY	☆☆☆☆☆
SERIES		COSTS	☆☆☆☆☆

COSTUME

SKETCH	ITEM	PRICE
	◯	
	◯	
	◯	
	◯	
	◯	
	◯	
	◯	
	◯	
	◯	
	◯	
	◯	
	◯	
	◯	
	◯	
	◯	

ADDITIONAL NOTES

DATE		PROJECT RATING	
TIME		EXPENDITURE	☆☆☆☆☆
CHARACTER		DIFFICULITY	☆☆☆☆☆
SERIES		COSTS	☆☆☆☆☆

COSTUME

SKETCH	ITEM	PRICE
	○	
	○	
	○	
	○	
	○	
	○	
	○	
	○	
	○	
	○	
	○	
	○	
	○	
	○	
	○	

ADDITIONAL NOTES

DATE	PROJECT RATING	
⊞ DATE		
⊙ TIME	🪡 EXPENDITURE	☆☆☆☆☆
🐯 CHARACTER	🧚 DIFFICULITY	☆☆☆☆☆
📽 SERIES	🎖 COSTS	☆☆☆☆☆

COSTUME

SKETCH	ITEM	PRICE
	○	
	○	
	○	
	○	
	○	
	○	
	○	
	○	
	○	
	○	
	○	
	○	
	○	
	○	
	○	

ADDITIONAL NOTES

DATE		PROJECT RATING	
TIME		EXPENDITURE	☆☆☆☆☆
CHARACTER		DIFFICULITY	☆☆☆☆☆
SERIES		COSTS	☆☆☆☆☆

COSTUME

SKETCH	ITEM	PRICE
	○	
	○	
	○	
	○	
	○	
	○	
	○	
	○	
	○	
	○	
	○	
	○	
	○	
	○	
	○	

ADDITIONAL NOTES

DATE		PROJECT RATING	
TIME		EXPENDITURE	☆☆☆☆☆
CHARACTER		DIFFICULITY	☆☆☆☆☆
SERIES		COSTS	☆☆☆☆☆

COSTUME

SKETCH	ITEM	PRICE
	○	
	○	
	○	
	○	
	○	
	○	
	○	
	○	
	○	
	○	
	○	
	○	
	○	
	○	
	○	

ADDITIONAL NOTES

DATE		PROJECT RATING	
TIME		EXPENDITURE	☆☆☆☆☆
CHARACTER		DIFFICULITY	☆☆☆☆☆
SERIES		COSTS	☆☆☆☆☆

COSTUME

SKETCH	ITEM	PRICE
	○	
	○	
	○	
	○	
	○	
	○	
	○	
	○	
	○	
	○	
	○	
	○	
	○	
	○	
	○	

ADDITIONAL NOTES

DATE		PROJECT RATING	
TIME		EXPENDITURE	☆☆☆☆☆
CHARACTER		DIFFICULITY	☆☆☆☆☆
SERIES		COSTS	☆☆☆☆☆

COSTUME

SKETCH	ITEM	PRICE
	○	
	○	
	○	
	○	
	○	
	○	
	○	
	○	
	○	
	○	
	○	
	○	
	○	
	○	
	○	

ADDITIONAL NOTES

DATE		PROJECT RATING	
TIME		EXPENDITURE	☆☆☆☆☆
CHARACTER		DIFFICULITY	☆☆☆☆☆
SERIES		COSTS	☆☆☆☆☆

COSTUME

SKETCH	ITEM	PRICE
	○	
	○	
	○	
	○	
	○	
	○	
	○	
	○	
	○	
	○	
	○	
	○	
	○	
	○	
	○	

ADDITIONAL NOTES

DATE		PROJECT RATING	

DATE

TIME

CHARACTER

SERIES

PROJECT RATING

EXPENDITURE ☆☆☆☆☆

DIFFICULITY ☆☆☆☆☆

COSTS ☆☆☆☆☆

COSTUME

SKETCH	ITEM	PRICE
	○	
	○	
	○	
	○	
	○	
	○	
	○	
	○	
	○	
	○	
	○	
	○	
	○	
	○	
	○	

ADDITIONAL NOTES

DATE		PROJECT RATING	
TIME		EXPENDITURE	☆☆☆☆☆
CHARACTER		DIFFICULITY	☆☆☆☆☆
SERIES		COSTS	☆☆☆☆☆

COSTUME

SKETCH	ITEM	PRICE
	○	
	○	
	○	
	○	
	○	
	○	
	○	
	○	
	○	
	○	
	○	
	○	
	○	
	○	
	○	

ADDITIONAL NOTES

DATE		PROJECT RATING	

📅 DATE
🕐 TIME
🧸 CHARACTER
🎬 SERIES

PROJECT RATING

🧵 EXPENDITURE	☆☆☆☆☆
✨ DIFFICULTY	☆☆☆☆☆
🎖 COSTS	☆☆☆☆☆

COSTUME

SKETCH	ITEM	PRICE
	○	
	○	
	○	
	○	
	○	
	○	
	○	
	○	
	○	
	○	
	○	
	○	
	○	
	○	
	○	

ADDITIONAL NOTES

DATE		PROJECT RATING	

DATE

TIME

CHARACTER

SERIES

PROJECT RATING

EXPENDITURE	☆☆☆☆☆
DIFFICULITY	☆☆☆☆☆
COSTS	☆☆☆☆☆

COSTUME

SKETCH	ITEM	PRICE
	○	
	○	
	○	
	○	
	○	
	○	
	○	
	○	
	○	
	○	
	○	
	○	
	○	
	○	
	○	

ADDITIONAL NOTES

DATE		PROJECT RATING	
TIME		EXPENDITURE	☆☆☆☆☆
CHARACTER		DIFFICULTY	☆☆☆☆☆
SERIES		COSTS	☆☆☆☆☆

COSTUME

SKETCH	ITEM	PRICE
	○	
	○	
	○	
	○	
	○	
	○	
	○	
	○	
	○	
	○	
	○	
	○	
	○	
	○	
	○	

ADDITIONAL NOTES

DATE		PROJECT RATING	
TIME		EXPENDITURE	☆☆☆☆☆
CHARACTER		DIFFICULITY	☆☆☆☆☆
SERIES		COSTS	☆☆☆☆☆

COSTUME

SKETCH	ITEM	PRICE
	○	
	○	
	○	
	○	
	○	
	○	
	○	
	○	
	○	
	○	
	○	
	○	
	○	
	○	
	○	

ADDITIONAL NOTES

DATE	PROJECT RATING		

📅 DATE	PROJECT RATING
🕐 TIME	🧵 EXPENDITURE ☆☆☆☆☆
🧸 CHARACTER	👗 DIFFICULTY ☆☆☆☆☆
🎬 SERIES	🏅 COSTS ☆☆☆☆☆

COSTUME

SKETCH	ITEM	PRICE
	○	
	○	
	○	
	○	
	○	
	○	
	○	
	○	
	○	
	○	
	○	
	○	
	○	
	○	
	○	

ADDITIONAL NOTES

DATE	PROJECT RATING	
TIME	EXPENDITURE	☆☆☆☆☆
CHARACTER	DIFFICULITY	☆☆☆☆☆
SERIES	COSTS	☆☆☆☆☆

COSTUME

SKETCH	ITEM	PRICE
	○	
	○	
	○	
	○	
	○	
	○	
	○	
	○	
	○	
	○	
	○	
	○	
	○	
	○	
	○	

ADDITIONAL NOTES

DATE		PROJECT RATING	

DATE			PROJECT RATING	
📅 DATE		🧵 EXPENDITURE	☆☆☆☆☆
🕐 TIME		💎 DIFFICULTY	☆☆☆☆☆
🎎 CHARACTER		🏅 COSTS	☆☆☆☆☆
🎬 SERIES			

COSTUME

SKETCH	ITEM	PRICE
	○	
	○	
	○	
	○	
	○	
	○	
	○	
	○	
	○	
	○	
	○	
	○	
	○	
	○	
	○	

ADDITIONAL NOTES

DATE	PROJECT RATING		
TIME	EXPENDITURE	☆☆☆☆☆	
CHARACTER	DIFFICULITY	☆☆☆☆☆	
SERIES	COSTS	☆☆☆☆☆	

COSTUME

SKETCH	ITEM	PRICE
	○	
	○	
	○	
	○	
	○	
	○	
	○	
	○	
	○	
	○	
	○	
	○	
	○	
	○	
	○	

ADDITIONAL NOTES

	DATE		PROJECT RATING	
	TIME		EXPENDITURE	☆☆☆☆☆
	CHARACTER		DIFFICULITY	☆☆☆☆☆
	SERIES		COSTS	☆☆☆☆☆

COSTUME

SKETCH	ITEM	PRICE
	○	
	○	
	○	
	○	
	○	
	○	
	○	
	○	
	○	
	○	
	○	
	○	
	○	
	○	
	○	

ADDITIONAL NOTES

Printed in Great Britain
by Amazon

31413081R00069